I0750294

FINISHING LINE PRESS
www.finishinglinepress.com

Yuba Witch

poems by

Meredith Heller

Finishing Line Press
Georgetown, Kentucky

Yuba Witch

To the Yuba River, always
My temple, my lover, my muse

Copyright © 2021 by Meredith Heller
ISBN 978-1-64662-624-3 First Edition
All rights reserved under International and Pan-American Copyright Conventions. No part of this book may be reproduced in any manner whatsoever without written permission from the publisher, except in the case of brief quotations embodied in critical articles and reviews.

ACKNOWLEDGMENTS

Special thanks to the generous editors of the following publications in which these poems first appeared, some in different versions.

Avocet—"Say Yes"
Common Ground—"Love's Forge"
Quiet Lightning—"Yuba Witch"
Raw Earth Ink—"Night Music"
Rebelle Society—"Burning Man," "Huntress of the Holy Sound," "Song of Summer," "Stories from Stones," "Summer's End"
Sad Girls Club—"Lady J"

Publisher: Leah Huete de Maines
Editor: Christen Kincaid
Cover Art: "I See Love," Arna Baartz, https://arnabaartz.com.au/
Author Photo: Meredith Heller
Cover Design: Elizabeth Maines McCleavy

Order online: www.finishinglinepress.com
also available on amazon.com

Author inquiries and mail orders:
Finishing Line Press
P. O. Box 1626
Georgetown, Kentucky 40324
U. S. A.

Table of Contents

Poetry, like witchcraft and magick,
is an act of transformation.
—Anaka Stucky, *from Literary Hub, March 3, 2019*

In summer of 2020, I left the world to go live on the South Fork of the Yuba River in Northern California. All summer I camped on the ground, without a tent, five feet from the water's edge to see if I could return to my essence. I'd had enough of the world for awhile, and then the pandemic hit, which exacerbated our isolation, separating us and adding to the ethos of us and them. I was in a constant state of grieving a society that has traded its heart for greed, territorialism, and materialism over felt experience, transcendence, and communion. We have fallen prey to consumption to fill the emptiness that can only be remedied with kindness and belonging.

I figured my greatest act of rebellion and my most direct path to salvation was to live as simply as possible, returning to the earth and elements to fill my holes, clean my wounds, atone my betrayals, and conjure my transformation.

Over the next few months, I fell so in love with the river and the wild creature I was becoming that one day I walked right into the jade water, voiced my vows, offered flower petals from the blackberry bushes growing near my camp, and stood tall, as the river encircled me in golden light, the rapids ringing glory. And in that moment, not *at* the river but *in* the river, we promised to be true to ourselves with each other.

Then she took me, under. As a poet, I did what I always do: allow myself to be moved by life, to translate the ineffable into words that strive to convey a moment—of oneness, gratitude, humility, liberation. And in the following months, the river did what she always does: flows downstream, teaching me how to let go.

Meredith Heller
Yuba River
California

Song of Summer

It was mid-June and the Maypole stood straight and strong in center field, wrapped in ribbons of prayers for the trees and the sky, the insects and four-leggeds, and oh, the people of this shining planet, breathing and birthing the new tribe, who live in harmony with the land and plant by the moon; seeding our future.

A young boy sat on the front steps of the porch in a straw hat, whistling while he watched her and a tiny black spider explored the edge of her paper, and the birds and insects claimed the day with their clamor, and the coffee went down smooth as brandy.

Hot in the heat of the kiln of the sun, I sat and I baked in the empire of the river, where cedar scents the air and the redwoods sing at the top of their lungs.

June, when the water still nips and the nights send me off for a sweater. It's not until July that the coo-coo comes calling, flying on her hollow bones, whistling a song of summer as I snake down the silver road to see who I'll become.

The garden of my bones had drained dry. I didn't know how sadness leaches the minerals from the soil, dissolving what matters, until the crystals of my wrist shattered, sounding an echo through the canyon, and I was asked to come lie down in the empty tunnels of my blood and reseed them with kindness.

So I planted flowers, purple and yellow, among dark leafy greens, and I placed rose-quartz at the center of my cells, and I waited, and I watered, while I bloomed.

Now I make time each day to ride a drumbeat like a horse galloping through the veil to the other side where the spirits come and place needles along my songlines until I hum, rub the gates of my feet and shoulders, my lower back, my belly, until I open and find the rhythm of my breath.

Bones to stones. Rock-a-bye, babe, the ancient voices sing from cradle to grave. God, we all just need to be held. Take off your shoes, sink the soles of your feet into the good earth, feel how your body opens to meet her. Your skin and sinew see more deeply than your eyes ever will. Grow quiet and slow enough to arrive in stillness and remember: *I am alive.*

Dream catchers and truth-sayers, woven like webs, strung up in the trees; each junction a jewel that sings, one thread to the next. Look in the grass there, an owl feather, juju from sweet land, where they hang leis on the graves by the side of the road.

You can't go back, Jack. North is the new south. The tavern of the lost and lonely is empty. Only ghosts whisper now as the door creaks closed and the red moon rises and the long snake stretches her back as you ride her curves, learning your own center.

Look for your name in the graffiti on the bridge, as the dreaded drum-boy slides by with a smile, his eyes like sun.

Sage shushes on the roadside as you walk past a sign for *MOONSHINE*, trusting we all find our own way home.

8:15am

I wondered
just when
it would happen

8:15am
sun comes trumpets
over the ridge

Ringing
my tiny postal
stamp

Nooked
into the river's
bend

Rapids sing glory
red dragonflies
scorch the air

I dive into liquid jade
let it lick the stars
from my skin

Celtic Knots

All day
my body
glued to granite
baking in the oven
of the sun

Unwinding Celtic knots
I tied when I was lonely
held me together
when I was broken

Each string
a prayer

I wait for the stars
excited as a child

Digging for Gold

With tools and pans
they pick and chisel
the veins for nuggets

Not fooled
by the sparkle of mica
they dig deeper for gold

Not knowing
how it offers itself
every morning

Singing
on the surface
of rock and rapid

Edward's Crossing

In summer
I come to the ashram
of the river

Golden-voiced water
plays songs on an old harpsichord
leaves her fingerprints on the keys
as she swirls downstream

I spend the morning
clearing a small footprint of sand
lifting and hauling rocks
building a dam
filling a shallow tub
for a warm bath

I slide in
water embraces me
in her jade hands
leaving no part of me
untouched

She welcomes me home
like a lover
returning from war
checks every part of me
for wounds and glory

Shows me her bounty ~
a row of ducklings
the brown osprey
black & white winged dragonflies
zigzagging on high wires

Three months of pandemic
shelter in place
hiatus of cars and wars and pollution

has done her well

Her lungs and skin are clear
her prana palpable

She lets me see through her eyes
I am humbled by the light

Stories from Stones

Day 1
The river glowed today
her face freckled with sun
she hummed and bubbled with a new song

She etched her name in circles on the rocks
laid her bare belly across their backs
and they drank the sorrow from her bones

What's underneath all the sadness? She wonders
What pulls everything into this dark eddy?

She touches the sadness with her finger
peels it away layer by layer
until she finds a young child
sitting alone on a rock
a full moon rising in her face
starfish growing in her hands
her heart longing for love

She teaches the child how to sing
to the music of the river
how to listen to the stories from stones
she shows her how to place her hand on her heart
and pledge her love to life

The wind blows through the child's hair
each tendril turns into a striped snake
that sings in its own language

Crickets gossip
the sky turns to smoke
slips into the water like a fish

It weaves a cord of copper rope
the child catches it
and spins like a dervish

The first star sparks the sky with flint
she breathes its white fire into her belly
bats swoop in jagged angles
above her head

The rocks lift their wizened faces to the sky
their eyes glinting with gold

She sleeps with the moon
curled on her side
her light spilling over

Day 2
It's after midnight
when they finally climb across the rock
into each other's bodies
between them grows
a creature with wings
that glow iridescent
in the moonlight

The creature catches a falling star
on the tip of its tongue

They sleep beneath the eyes of the stars
while the water creature
mumbles prayers
into their ears

Day 3
Morning wakes them
by strumming a few chords
of color across the sky

Tall pines breathe above them
the river roars with joy

Her friend slinks up the canyon
leaving her in the bright hands of morning

She swims in the river
the sun drinks water droplets from her skin
like a child licking an ice-cream cone

She melts into the granite boulder
that holds her against its body
like a lover

Just me and the river, she thinks
the air humming with dragonflies
the only words left in her mouth are,
Thank You.

Day 4
All night and all morning
the river and I flow downstream
sharing love songs

Under water, stones gather
in patterns of sacred geometry
pushed and pulled
by the magnetics of their minerals
aligning along invisible threads
that hum with life

Yuba River
your veins filled with gold
you lick me with your mossy tongue
your own skin rippling
as I lose my edges
dissolve into the sun
come out the other side

Truth

The truth is—
Evening
is my favorite time
at the river

All the people go home
Everything grows quiet

I can hear the river singing
I can feel her
breathing

Setting sun
tilts the light
apricot cloud-fish
chase each other
through gilded water

Bats flutter
like dark butterflies
taking bites
out of
the ripe
moon

Tilting the Horizon

It's happening!

The sky is swimming
   pink and blue fish
chase each other
   across the river's surface
catch each
   other's reflection
before they dive under
   dragonflies
tilting the horizon
   rocks taking off
their stone masks
   unfolding their limbs
stretching their gray bodies
   into the water
and watching me
   with their creature eyes

Heartbeat

Morning news burbles downstream
under a waning moon hanging
in a blue hammock sky

Dragonflies iridesce in sunlight
swinging crazy circles
on invisible trapeze

Siren songs rise
and *wongle*
on the wind

Water dancers undulate
to afternoon drums
pulsing

Like a heartbeat
from the ventricles
of the red parachute tent

And Obo takes me
to see
where the sun

Is building
a fire
on the rock

Gloaming

If you look
from a certain
corner of your eye
you may see
the moon-faced
Buddhas
who live in the rocks

Who throw you a twinkle
and a kiss
before retreating
to their hovel
where the council
has commenced

If you tilt your ear
to the space
between the notes
of the rapids
you may hear
the Selkies
singing
in the serpentine

Clean is the granite
that reflects the sun
on the palms
of the planet
as we orbit

Wind churns the water
traces her fingers
at the border
where the gloaming
approaches
with grace

Obo

Obo coyote comes calling
in a pink snow suit
he skips rocks
scratches his red beard
smiles from green-flower eyes
collects words in his pockets
talks to faeries
spins stories
on an old Martin guitar
swings
from the strings
of the moon

Like You Said in Your Song

—For Obo

You found me
here in the nook
at the river's bend
I was hiding out

No bower, you asked?
Nope, just out in the open
under the stars
tucked into bed
glooming about
an old wizard friend
who lost his charm

We shared songs
and an imaginary bottle
of pear cider
each of us quenching
our own version
of Sergeant Pepper's
Lonely Hearts Club Band
you in costume, of course

As the gloaming crept in
my edges softened
and right after you hiked
up the hill

The slowest star
I've ever seen
dripped
down
the
sky

And like you said in your song:
Thank You & I'm Sorry
both engender
a journey
of tears

Night Music

Sun woke me
hot handing
my shoulder

River already up
chattering
night too short

Jester in a blue jumpsuit
begged off at dusk
chasing the comet

Left me
with bats
in the belfry

Rhyming myself
into a tangle
until the wee hours

And just when I'd nodded off
skunk came snuffling
for peanuts & blueberries & other treasures

And the star-animals turned
on their dark carousel
cranking the night music

Say Yes

At midnight on Tuesday
her flower bloomed
beside the river
that pours in pulses of lace
through the eye holes
of the rock skulls
that rest their heads
on the bank to dream

She cracks and crumbles
into the murmur of water
that signs its name
across her skin
delicately devouring her edges
until even her essence
dissolves

The granite boulders of her back
marbled with grief
break apart at the seams
scatter the water
with sparks
from her veins

Say yes to an invitation from Hades
received on a handwritten scroll
tied with a white string
hidden in a rock crevice
and read one evening
as the moon
sliced the sky

She remembers
one humid summer night
when she stayed out late
with the boy who read a book
under the street lamp

while bats darted in and out
catching moths
in their mouths

Language was a song she sang
as she rode her bike
up and down the hill
a melody tattooed its signature
across her shoulders
in notes she bent
on the lute of her ribs
Her polka dot shirt unbuttoned
flying in the breeze behind her

Resist Resistance
She sings to herself
like a mantra

Her supple spine
rises toward the light
as she spins on a tilted axis
from gravity's hip

The water takes and turns her
in its wise white hands
as she composts
last year's loss

In the morning
a velvet peach
ripens in her throat
she warbles as she's born

Year after year
of dark nights
and bright noon-tides
the zippered pocket

of her being
opens
and
closes

Native Tongue

During the day
the rocks sleep

crumpled creatures
hiding in the light

but come night
they wake

shake out
the shadows

open their
ancient eyes

drink
the darkness

chanting
in their native tongue

Blue Damselflies

Sister river
you welcome me home
hold me in your rock cradles
wash my feet and face
knead my shoulders
in your stone hot hands

Wind licks dust
from my worry lines
rushing water
clears the chatter
from my brain

Blue damselflies
mate on my belly

Has it been only a week I was gone?

Days pass so quickly in the world
I run to keep up

But here
in your effervescent valley
I slow to a deeper rhythm

The ancient animal
who sleeps inside my bones
crawls to the surface
gulping the air

River Sirens

The river sirens
are singing songs
in Spanish
strumming an old guitar
sipping wine from the bottle
as the earth spins

I offer up a melody
in harmony
to the chorus
of the rapids

Asking forgiveness
as I sift through my past
stirring the silt
shaking the pan
weighing the gold

I promise to write a few letters
to people I've wronged

There is atonement at the river
if you surrender to the water

Allow her to have her way with you

She'll teach you
how
to let go

Last Hot Kiss

A pilgrimage of people
arrives at the river
bodies all shades and sizes
decorated in ink
find their niche
in sun-painted rocks
their bodies and the rocks
indistinguishable
in late afternoon glow
as children jack-knife
off rock perches
and lovers kiss

Moms float babies downstream
cradled in bright inner tubes
slap-happy dogs paddle the water
a yellow swallowtail
floats by on paper wings

what if instead of cursing the guy
with the boombox
I simply say, *Yes to this moment, too*
or I migrate somewhere quieter
with a smile on my face
or like the sirens
I sing louder

I find a spot of shade
mold the arch of my back
into soft sand
and await the golden hour
when the river will reflect
the sun's rosy cheeks

and the world
will melt and fuse

like glass
in the last hot kiss
from the sun’s kiln

The Fey

Don't go painting purple
marks on the trees
pointing your people
to secret places
where you get free

The fey will find you!

Divine you
friend or foe
cover your graffiti
with bark and moss
and things that grow

And your friends will get lost!

The river will swallow what ails you
your inner sense will wake you
you'll shed an old self or two

Your skin
will become a living thing
and the animal who lives
in your bones
will come home
to sing

Come Up for Air

After you've beat yourself
to a fine powder

after you've kicked his memory
clear into the next galaxy

after you've poked
every wound

on the map
of your psyche

ground every sore spot
against a rock

until you see red.
There is a moment

when something bigger than you
picks you up

by the scruff of your neck
and offers you

another choice.
To soften

into the edge
of what hurts

to trust life
to guide you

to allow yourself
to slow down enough

to truly feel

what you feel

and then
to let it go

into the river
to be washed

home to the sea
where the salt

turns everything back
to its original nature

and the hurt will melt
like ice in the sun

and the forms your pain took
will no longer matter

and will you sit
with yourself

broken
open

and you will pick yourself up
dive into the jade water

watch the dragonflies
diagonate the sky

and you will
come up for air

Two Avocados

I offered a bag of carrots
to a homeless man
in the parking lot
but he said he had no teeth
to chew them

So I brought two avocados
he opened a hand
as wide & dry
as the Mojave desert
and thanked me

Before rolling himself
back into his cigarette
and the companionship
of smoke

Tell It To The River

The barn on Travilah Road
along the Potomac River in Maryland
where I made a home at 13
slept on the floor
with an old sleeping bag
from Salvation Army
hung a torn lace curtain
in the window
where the glass had been broken
long ago

I ate stale rye bread
from the trash
spent my quarters
on a tin of Medaglia d'Oro coffee
dark & sweet
like the beekeeper boy
I kissed behind the hive
for a jar of local honey
my skin buzzing,

Tell it to the river

I was 15
living in a log cabin
in the foothills
of the Blue Ridge Mountains, Virginia
no electricity
no running water
with Willy, 28
who kicked around
in a pair of red converse hightops
pinned me to the hood of his station wagon
and held his hand over my mouth
so no one would hear me scream,

Tell it to the river

I made bracelets
from copperhead snakes
I found dead on the road
taught myself to tan their skins
by slicing them open
scooping out their guts
once I found a baby bird inside
once a handful of fleshy eggs

I'd nail the skins
to a wooden board
salt them and leave them
to dry in the sun
cut the skin into strips
sew them around a piece of rope
attached to a tube of beads I made
in a pattern called peyote stitch
I learned from the women
on the Navaho Reservation
I'd sell the bracelets in town for 20 bucks
which was a lot of food money
back then,

Tell it to the river

The boy I met one summer
whose skin was made
of cinnamon
who sat all day
at the water's edge
singing in a language
no one knew but me
we watched the water
braid the light
in helixes
we made love
in a circle of pines

under a full moon
and they found his body
three days later
I crawled inside myself
and didn't speak
for many months
when I was a teen
on my own
trading my sex
for survival
my love
for belonging,

Tell it to the river

My friend Annelies
85 year-old Swiss artist
who simply is not old
she is tiny and strong
and determined as a beetle
hands constantly
making things
come to life
paper and glass
paint and clay

She keeps bees
feeds the raccoons
cheats at cards
cusses worse than I do
when she loses
yodels expertly
and rides downhill
every morning
on her kick-scooter
to swim in the pool
a smile on her face

She was my first true friend
she found me
when I was a lone wolf
my skin chewed raw
my fur full of sparks
slowly she shaped me
like one of her clay pots
into a human being
with a space inside
for homemade soup,

Tell it to the river

To all the bards
along my path
who wonder where I go
when I go
who know me
as the wolf-hearted woman
with one eye dark
and one eye bright
one eye that looks inward
one that looks out
one that draws you closer
while the other
pushes you away,

Tell it to the river

The way the water
loosens my hinges
turns my blood to opals
throws herself against me
purring like some wild beast
I rest my head against her chest
listen to her heartbeat:

yes, now
yes, now

The sun climbs the ridge
in the morning
and we howl together
because it's good to be alive
and say so,

Tell it to the river

Wishing Well

Wishing well
stones like copper pennies
tossed by faeries
tumbled by two boys
who shuffle-foot
across stepping stones
with treasure
in their hands

Carved by Picasso

Picasso was here
carving stone
long before
the gold miners

He etched curves
smooth as skin
cubed contours
of body & bone
chiseled edges
jagged with pain
puzzled them
against the sky

Only the water watched
with her millions of eyes
singing & shining
as he worked the rock

She, knowing the patience
and persistence it takes
to whittle the surface
reveal the essence

Balancing force
without forcing

Drone Tone

—For Jeannie McKenzie & Tiffiny Fyans
My river singsong sisters

We droned
until the overtones
found us
until we kneeled
on the ground
and the voices
sang
all around us

Speaking in Tongues

I tucked my body deep
into a rock cranny
where rapids roil
bubbles churn
and dragons dervish
in the suds

The river rumbled
speaking in tongues

I heard light
sparkling
in cacophony

I saw a chorus
of chaos
it erased all thought

It taught me
an indigenous language

Where grief surfaces
and sobs rhythmically
in cycles
wise as water
repeatedly
until it comes
clean

Gold Coins

Right before dusk
the sun slips loose
dances downstream
throwing handfuls
of gold coins
for the vagabonds
on the banks
who chase them
as they spiral the water
like music

I follow the trail
of sparks
into a pool
of smoky quartz
it swallows me
whole

Underwater
there are villages
of fish & stone

I join them
as they haggle
at market
pray at temple

I stay under
as long as I can
searching for a mate
but I run out of air

I float to the surface
just in time
to catch a butterfly
shadow dancing
across the rock face

Jump Rope

You know you're almost there
when the road turns tightly
gravel gives way to dirt

A scent ancient as earth
tugs at your brain
like a lost childhood song

You scramble to catch
along a threadbare melody
looping like jump rope

Huntress of the Holy Sound

I sat by the river
and I listened to the water

she was singing about forgiveness
she was singing about hunger

she was singing a song of sunlight
as my body rolled under

I asked the rocks
I asked the water

what to do about my hunger
while I chewed

on rinds of anger
by the mouth of the river

she sat down beside me
touched my skin with her fingers

shake out your bones
you wild creature

shake out your bones
you wild dancer

gather and empty
your blood of what aches

and the moon
will make her honey

in the dark
from your mistakes

I sat by the river
I listened to the water

her waves washed me over
like the hands of the mother

I came clean to her gospel
I came hard to her thunder

her waves washed me over
as my body rolled under

let go your worries
lay your body down

here at the river
where the earth is hallowed ground

let go your worries
lay your body down

the gospel of the water
will unwind what is bound

light a flame for forgiveness
light a flame for truth

claim your worthiness of love
grow into your youth

come home to the river
home to this sacred sound

where the water sings your name
in the secret language that you found

there are circles on the water
playing prism with the light

there are rocks carved with faces
who tell your fortune in the night

she will wrap you in her rapture
share her pockets treasures deep

your tears will turn to temples
in the healing of her heat

she'll sing a song of forgiveness
in a hard-earned melody

her music will absolve you
of every wrongful deed

whisper your prayers to the water
moan your desire to the moon

turn your wisdom into soil
seeds to plant, seeds to bloom

come home to the river
home to this holy ground

the gospel of the water
will wash your body down

come home to the river
lay your body down

feed the bones of your past
to the mouth of this holy ground

sit here by the water
hear your name in her song

come clean to her rhythm
here where you belong

Desert Dakini

Desert dakini
chants hymns
at dusk
rolls dry leaves
across her tongue
like dice
dances
with the wind
her eyes closed
her breath
like sagebrush
as she leans
against your body
and your skin loosens
to let her in

Smoke & Ash

After the Jones Bridge Fire 2020

The river is choked
smoke & ash
clog her lungs
she slides downstream
keeping the faith
but I can tell
she's weary

She's lost her shine
her skin is sallow with soot

Even the fish are gray
their translucent bodies
once glinting with gold
now dart like shadows
through narrow alleys
stealing the light

Come a good winter rain
a lush spring snowmelt
cleanse and replenish
this scarred canyon womb
make her fertile and fecund
singing her gospel
in the morning glory

Osprey

Sprawled on a rock
in the sun
I had almost dissolved
into nothingness
when the osprey
came winging
dapper in his tweed jacket
and white beret
whistling a greeting
on his clarinet
he perched on a dead branch
surveying his kingdom
of smoke & ash

Sepia Haze

In sepia haze
burnt flame floats
on water's surface

like a mirage

Honey-dipped disk
slides down behind ridge
veiled in smoke & ash

Burnished fingers
taking the world
with it

Love's Forge

I thought she'd risen
fair and square
from the final fires

I thought all the birds
had broken through their shells
flown in dark spirals
to their own side of the moon

I thought Spring had spread her wings
and dripping with dew
pulled her daughters up
from rain-quenched soil

I thought she'd finally broken open
shook her skin like a snake
until she came clean

But Fate, that slippery fish
swam against the tide
shattering the light
with his shadow

He stopped her in her tracks
one Sunday afternoon
chewed his way right through her wrist
pieces of her flesh stuck between his teeth

Bound her with a metal plate
screwing her into place
until she dismembered her past

~

In the forge of her will
she melted herself down

In the white hot heat
the last glowing embers
of survival
rolled over
in surrender

~

I heard she drank the fire
I heard she tempered her sword
I heard she sat in stillness
until peace found her

I heard her heart remembered to belong
I heard she tuned her compass
to a new wilderness
where each moment sings

Birthday Candles

Morning birds fly in
their bodies bright
as birthday candles

The river rows
her nimble boat
downstream

Navigating rocks
singing
her sunrise aria

Clouds
crochet
the morning

In a white wool shawl
that slips slowly
off her shoulder

As the sun finesses
his fingers
into her every nook

Around the Next Bend

Around the next bend
is a blackberry bush
pink flowers
and ripe berries
baked with sun

Feast
until your fingers
and mouth
are purpled
with pleasure

Climb up
the rock perch
in the shade
watch the water
spill in torrents

Allow the heat
of the rocks
to melt
the tension
in your back

Let the sound
of the current
sweep
your blood
clean

And then,
the blue heron

Lady J

—For Jennifer Harding, Feb 14, 1966—Sept 19, 2010

I only have one photo of you
you are sitting in my house in Boulder, Colorado

mid-sentence, your hands lift like birds
a small nest of fire burning in each palm

you're holding court on the pillows of Esmeralda
our eight-foot long, lime green velveteen sofa

we bought at a yard sale on 5th & Arapahoe for thirty bucks
because you said it would invite tall men to lie down

we met because we kept seeing each other around town wearing each other's
old jeans we managed to squeeze into at the consignment store

you finally suggested we get together and do a clothing swap
so we could stop paying for each other's hand-me-downs

I came over to your apartment by the creek, above the old roadhouse
and you put acupuncture needles in my arm

we dressed up for each other every day after that, sassy cabaret-cowgirls
in aubergine-colored jeans, bad-ass boots, vintage silk camisoles

we realized we were more sisters than we were strangers
and we were inseparable for the next five years

until we broke up because you told me I didn't know what God was
and if I had it to do again now, I would've just laughed at you

rather than walking away because how could I not know
what God was when you always amazed me

you who wore lingerie under your Catholic school uniform
so you had something to smile about when the nuns beat you down

you who showed me how to afford to eat in Boulder:
If you put it in a brown paper bag at the market, Lady M,

you can put whatever price you want on it!
nothing major: heirloom tomatoes, organic cherries, dark chocolate haystacks

you who would call me at 10pm on trash night
and say, *Come on Lady M, time to go alley shopping!*

and we'd fill the back of your beater truck with treasures we pirated from
the dumpsters both of us finding whatever we needed to furnish our homes

you who directed me to College in Vermont
where I learned my own worth

you who asked me how I bring my poems to life
and accompanied me to do my first public reading, my hands and voice shaking

you who shamelessly ate boxes of chocolate chip cookies
in your white silk kimono while scribbling haiku

you who could turn any concern I had on its head
by asking me to look at it another way

and your wisest line to me, *Well, Lady Meredith,*
the rules only apply to you if you let them

I miss you, Lady J
I never got to say goodbye when you were dying

we had drifted apart and old grudges kept us that way
I didn't find out until a year later

you came to me in a dream one mid-September night
when you didn't answer my calls or emails, I searched you up

found your obituary, stunned, I asked questions
the answer came too late, pancreatic cancer

I went for a walk that night, one year from the day you died
and I swear you came with me

said you were ready to move on
and I was the only one you hadn't spoken with

and then there was this moment
when you let me to see through your eyes

everywhere I looked all the molecules
glowed like millions of tiny suns

I stood there transfixed
you said, *This is what it REALLY looks like, Lady M*

and then it was over
and you were gone

and it was too late to tell you
that I had seen your hands lift like firebirds

that the scenes on your kimono came to life
and danced in luminous poetry

Night Boys

The night boys
skip stones
and munch mushrooms
under the stars

Snake charmer
finds his key
opens my heart
with the high notes of his flute

Starman leaps & lounges
on the rocks
plants a sunflower sprout
in a circle of stones

Eats chocolate from my fingers
spins stories & songs
that pull me in like a lasso
and would've tied me to my tears

But I saw his rose quartz star
chipped at the edges
leaving sharp shards
in the sand

So I walked away
but not before he left
his kiss imprinted
across my poem

The way we leave
our essence
to weather in the wind
like a prayer flag

Vincent

Vincent visited the river today
tall and lean
head shaved clean
he sat in full lotus
meditating
while the longhaired
cannabis-smoking hipsters
pranced across the rocks
their pixie girlfriends
bouncing barebreasted
chittering to each other
across the water

Vincent was silent
all discipline and poise
the only movement
his tattoos
hissing like snakes
across his skin

All day he sat quietly
and watched the river
a band of black ink
penned across his eyes
like a blindfold
but he saw through

I played a song on guitar and sang,

Wake me when you're ready
I'll just be here dreaming
Wake me when you're ready to go

He stood and bowed
hands pressed in prayer
eyes met mine
lucid as sky

I noticed his belt buckle
a silver octopus
dancing dervish
Cool buckle, I said
He replied with a huge grin, and one word:
~ *CRACKING!*

I saw him only once more that summer
I was walking back from Emerald Pools
and I spied him turning down the trail
toward Oak Tree
I made a soft animal sound
and he stopped in his tracks
turning slowly, he smiled

I shared that I'd just had an extraordinary experience
I'd fallen asleep on the rocks
and dreamed I'd grown a mermaid's tail
scales shimmering in the sun
undulating with a life of its own
rocking me into rhythm
with the universe

How about you? I asked
What? he replied
Um, I said, *anything extraordinary?*

His eyes shone like two small oceans
connected by a border of ink
that tethered his face to a dark past

He said, *it already is.*

Burning Man

Biking across the moon
a temple of infinite white
an ancient river bed
belly scalloped and scaled
by fossilized fish
and creatures who make pearls
in the darkness
underground

The wind is my compass
she leads me in circles
wraps me in silks
whispers in vibrato
until my rusty gates
swing open

Surrender to the dust
all day and all night
the white witch
sugars my skin

Follow her silver trails
that trace my body like a map
revealing each crevice
where I push or pull
toward or against the grain
where I stretch
on the bias

The doors of the desert
open to let me in
I turn on a kaleidoscope
of color and sound
one heart pulsing
spinning dust devils
blowing a song
on didgeridoo

I dervish through worm holes
into spaces of stillness
where for one brief moment
I am held in the palm of her hand
offered a cool drink from her oasis
and billowing with gratitude
I spill into everything
and nothingness
all at once

Dawn in the desert
licks the sky
with her pastel tongue

Moon drips
the last bead of honey
from the tip of her scythe
into the horizon's fold

Pirate ships
that roam the riverbed
sail home
with their carousel horses
and Coney Island neon

Here in the desert
civilizations rise and die
leaving no trace
of their love
and their loss
totems crumble and fall
in the fire
that is speaking
in tongues

I am tempered
in the forge of the sun

heated and cooled
hammered and folded
over and over
until the inside of me
and the outside of me
meet and merge

I see between the particles
to the space
that connects us all

We are the makers
the specks that glow
in this great sea

Leaving only an echo
as we sign our names
in the dust

Which we too
will become

Yuba Witch

Muscle by muscle
bone by bone
she takes herself apart

scrubs her heart
in the river
grinds the knot

in her back
against the stones
dives under the water

holds her breath
letting the river's
mossy tongue

taste her
until her lungs
beg for air

CHOOSE
chants
the river

She opens her eyes
underwater
looks down at her body

watches it rippling
in waves of light
it would be so easy

to dissolve
she hears the sun
singing above her

feels her heart
beat in unison
she cuts the tether

rises to the surface
shedding the water
like a snake skin

she swims to shore
bleeds iron
from the stones

oils her joints
climbing up & down
the rocks

guzzles from the spring
quenching
her thirst

bakes herself copper
in the sun
until the current

runs through her
clear as the first flutes
of morning

every molecule
awake
to the music

the river rushing
over the rocks
singing in gospel

the choir of the pines
rehearsing
a requiem

~

She leans back onto hot granite
her legs open to the sun
her vulva wet

the last wild blackberry
of summer
in her mouth

dragonflies
sailing
the wind

Summer's End

Weather's changing, water's two degrees cooler than last week, wind's picked up. The days grow shorter which means I have to make each moment last longer. Mystic and the muppet-boys are here today, partying. They cozy up right next to the two new forest nymphs, morning giggle girls, who spin late night stories on a fiddle, while River Dave sings his heart out and tells me, *Today is more Van Gogh than Monet.*

Shadow-girl scoops melon balls on the beach and hands them out like festive fire-crackers. We suck the juice from their salmon-colored hearts and cheer the explosion in our mouths. The dragonflies are either fat or pregnant tonight, or maybe like me, they've stuffed themselves on every summer sparkle, and now they're drunken and swaying on iridescent high-wires above the river's shining face, the sun's blush tucked into her smile lines.

Lady Bones sat with me on the big rock today and we talked vulvas. The importance of keeping ours juicy and vital. And I thought, *it's time!* It's been a whole year since I broke my heart on that damn bird-man. Highest I ever flew; hardest I've fallen in years. At least I wrote one good new song, and he gave me his travel guitar with the Nashville tuning. We dubbed our duo: *The Dirty Love Birds.*

I'm feeling inspired today. I'm gonna get me some sex. And if not for love, then for the plain fucking health of my cunt. Today I found this place under a big rock where the shadows live. I watched for a long time as dusk settled on the sand and I wondered if any light would sing there, but it only grew darker and drank up what was left of the day.

I felt the first pang of summer's end, the way the darkness begins to outshine the light. Rocks and trees blur into their nighttime creatures. I curl up on the big rock to absorb the last heat before the night chills. I consider going to town to hear Cricket play banjo but the night chorus here at the river roots me to the ground and the August full moon calls me by name.

I set up my bed under the striped canopy and thank the universe for keeping this whole crazy circus spinning. I'm grateful there are still places like this where we can get naked, swim in the river, drink from a spring, sleep outside with the whole damn cosmos pulsing.

And I vow in this life that I will not become jaded. Sleeping outside still thrills me. I don't know exactly what we are or why we're here, but I do know I have the courage to keep loving.

And living here, woven into nature, the water washing my bones clean, the trees teaching me how to breathe, is still the best medicine I know.

Lady Yuba

It was late season at the river, mid-November, too cold to put my body in the water, but spending six or seven hours scrambling up and down rocks along the bank from one end to the other still made me deliriously happy.

There wasn't another soul out there along my favorite stretch of the south fork, just me and the river, and I followed my nose along an intuitive trail, letting my body guide me.

I tested my strength and balance by climbing rock faces, navigating boulders, trusting tree bridges. I fell in love with oval-shaped stones and water-sculpted wood.

I stopped to build cairns, carefully stacking each new stone, listening for an etheric bell that rings when balance finds its seat. River yoga. I'd been exploring for a few hours when I popped around a bend and felt summoned into a rock nook.

And there she was! *Lady Yuba.* A life-size woman's torso carved from a driftwood log. She was leaning against a wall of lichen-covered rock under a canopy of thatched branches. Anatomically lovely, reigning over her river.

I wanted to take her home, but besides the fact that she was too heavy, she didn't belong to me; she belonged to the river. I was so stunned at even finding her. I snapped a few photos and sat down next to her to commune.

Questions flooded my brain: Who made her? How long has she been here? Has anyone else seen her? Did her creator camp out here all summer carving until she was finished?

I realized that this winter when the water rises higher than my head is now, she will be lifted up and carried downstream by an unforgiving current. It gave me chills knowing that I am most likely the last person to see her before her journey.

Will she survive the wild ride of winter's current and be spit out like a seed in spring? Or will the elements devour her?

I felt like the luckiest girl on earth to have just happened upon her. She, a spirit of the Yuba River, brought to life by a selfless artist who I imagine flirted with the existential paradox of ephemerality.

I kissed her neck, her heart, her belly. And I walked back down the river knowing that this world is full of fleeting magic.

Lady Yuba

Meredith Heller is a poet, singer/songwriter, educator, and author of *Write a Poem, Save Your Life* and three poetry collections. A California Poet in the Schools, she leads workshops for grades 1-12 in public and private schools, Juvenile Detention Centers, Women's Prisons, and online for women and teens. She is avid nature-woman who spends her summers camping beside rivers and oceans. She lives with a gentle footprint in a tinyhome in Northern California. For info about her workshops: www.meredithheller.com

www.ingramcontent.com/pod-product-compliance
Lightning Source LLC
LaVergne TN
LVHW051018080826
845145LV00009B/2683

* 9 7 8 1 6 4 6 6 2 6 2 4 3 *